AF575856

AMERICAN PIT BULL TERRIER

BY CORINNE FICKETT

TABLE OF CONTENTS

A Crabtree Seedlings Book

Crabtree Publishing
crabtreebooks.com

School-to-Home Support for Caregivers and Teachers

This book helps children grow by letting them practice reading. Here are a few guiding questions to help the reader with building his or her comprehension skills. Possible answers appear here in red.

Before Reading:

- What do I think this book is about?
  - *I think this book is about American Pit Bull Terriers.*
  - *I think this book is about bully breeds.*

- What do I want to learn about this topic?
  - *I want to learn about the American Pit Bull Terrier's characteristics.*
  - *I want to know why the American Pit Bull Terrier is a bully breed.*

During Reading:

- I wonder why...
  - *I wonder why a Pit Bull needs a firm and confident trainer.*
  - *I wonder why Pit Bulls are good search-and-rescue dogs.*

- What have I learned so far?
  - *I have learned that Pit Bulls have muscular bodies.*
  - *I have learned that a Pit Bull's coat can be a solid color or brindle.*

After Reading:

- What details did I learn about this topic?
  - *I have learned that Pit Bulls are very smart.*
  - *I have learned that bully breeds come from Molosser dogs.*

- Read the book again and look for the vocabulary words.
  - *I see the word breed on page 3, and the word muscular on page 4. The other glossary words are found on pages 22 and 23.*

The American Pit Bull Terrier, or Pit Bull, is a bully **breed**.

Neapolitan Mastiff

All bully breeds come from Molosser dogs. These dogs were large and **muscular**.

FUN FACT

Molosser dogs came from Greece.

Like other bully breeds, Pit Bulls have muscular bodies.

They also have **broad** chests.

A Pit Bull's coat is short, flat, and smooth.

It can be a solid color or **brindle**.

Most Pit Bulls weigh 30 to 80 pounds (13 to 36 kilograms). They stand 18 to 19 inches (45 to 48 centimeters) tall.

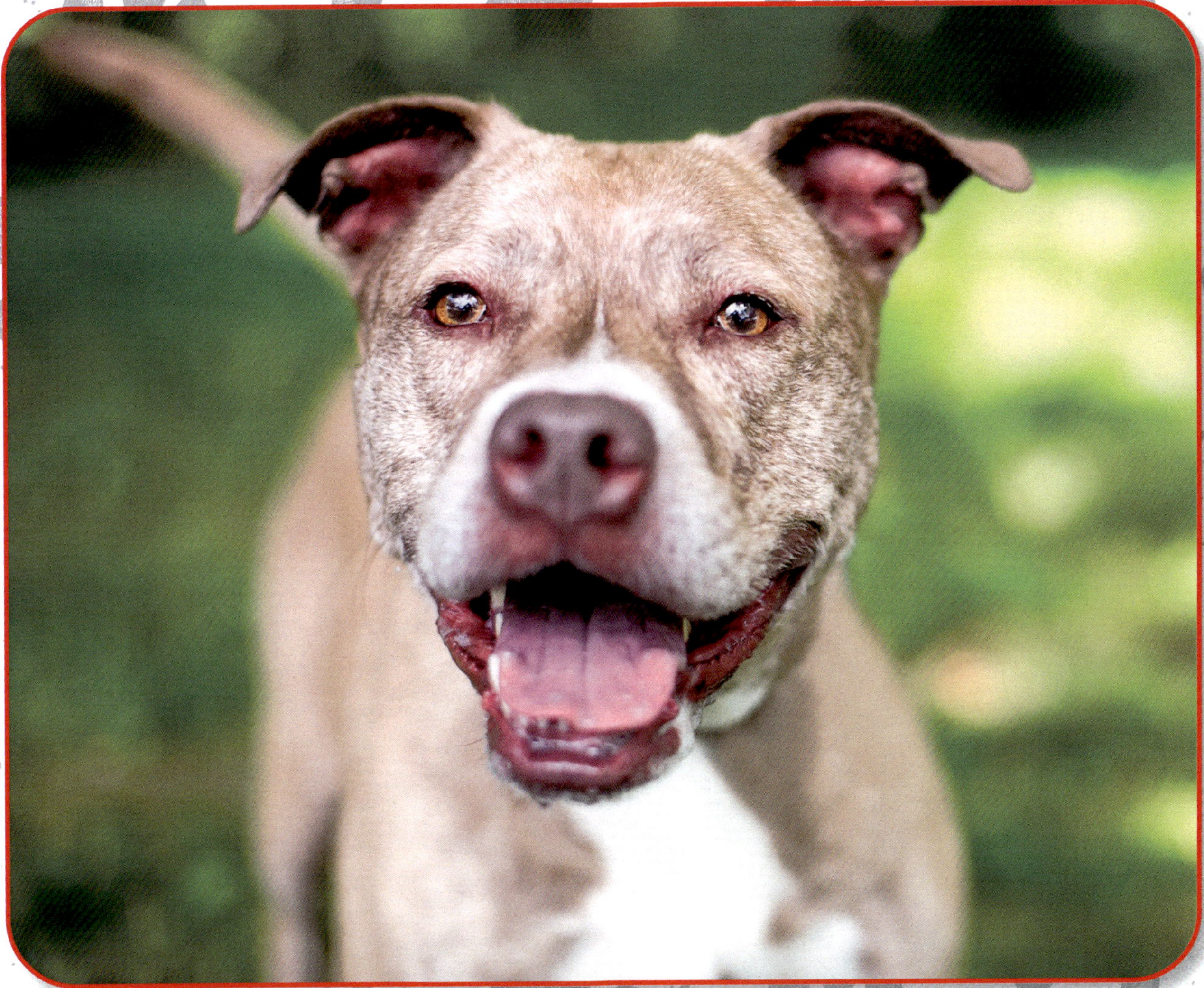

A Pit Bull's average life span is 12 to 14 years.

Pit Bulls are **loyal** to their human families.

Compared to other breeds, they may be less friendly with other dogs.

Pit Bulls are very smart and like to learn. They need a firm and confident trainer.

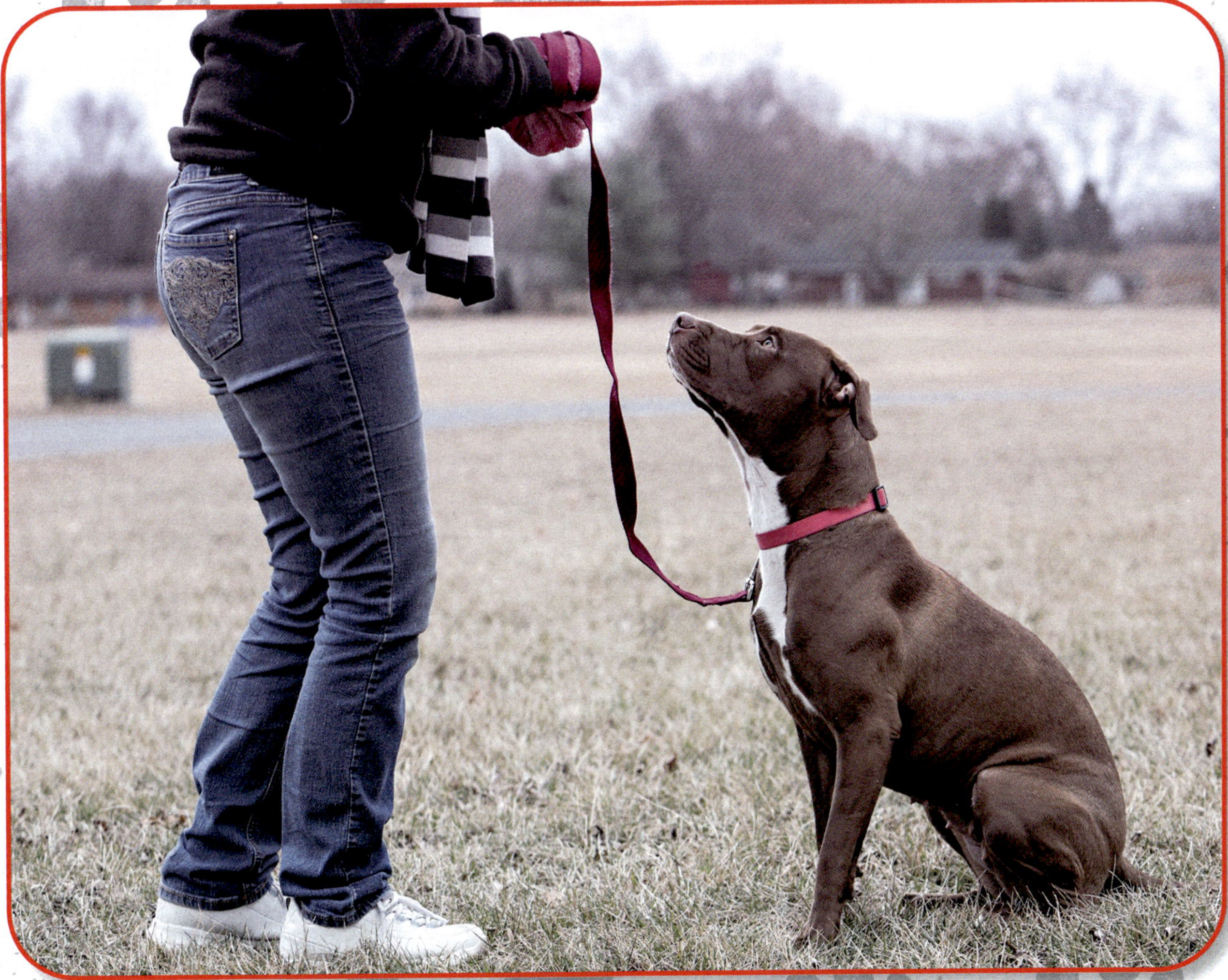

FUN FACT

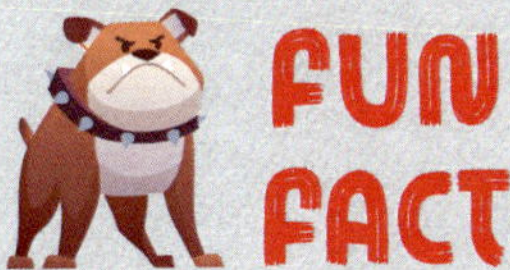

Training a Pit Bull is a good bonding experience.

NFL Quarterback Patrick Mahomes owns a Pit Bull named Steel.

Some Pit Bulls are trained to become **search-and-rescue** dogs.

An American Pit Bull Terrier can be a great addition to the right family.

Am I Ready to Adopt a Dog?

Adopting a dog is a big responsibility. It is important for you and your family to be fully prepared and committed to providing the best possible care for your furry friend. Take this quiz to see if you and your family are ready to talk about getting a dog.

1. Do you know that dogs require a lot of attention and care? **Yes / No**
2. Are you willing to spend time playing, walking, and interacting with a dog every day? **Yes / No**
3. Do you understand that dogs need regular feeding, grooming, and visits to the veterinarian? **Yes / No**
4. Are you patient enough to train a dog and teach them basic commands like sit, stay, and come? **Yes / No**
5. Is your household free of dog allergies? **Yes / No**
6. Do you have enough space in your home and an area for a dog to move around and play? **Yes / No**
7. Can you commit to caring for a dog for its entire life span? **Yes / No**
8. Are you prepared to clean up after the dog, including picking up its poop? **Yes / No**
9. Can you handle the financial responsibility of providing food, toys, medical care, and other necessities for the dog? **Yes / No**
10. Do you understand that dogs need regular socialization with other dogs and people to stay happy and well-behaved? **Yes / No**
11. Are you willing to commit to taking care of a dog during busy times or vacations? **Yes / No**
12. Can you handle the challenges of training and caring for a dog, even when things get tough? **Yes / No**

Determine your score by adding up all the "yes" answers.

10–12 Yes answers: You are ready to begin a conversation about adopting a dog.
6–9 Yes answers: You might be ready to think about adopting a dog.
0–5 Yes answers: You are not ready to take on the huge responsibility of adopting a furry friend.

Myths About Bully Breeds

Myth 1

Bully breeds are the most dangerous types of dogs.

Studies have not found that bully breeds are more dangerous than other types of dogs. The American Veterinary Medical Association (AVMA) states that any dog can bite. A dog's individual history and situation determines how likely it is to bite.

Myth 2

Bully breeds can lock their jaws.

No dog breed is able to "lock" its jaws. Usually, larger dogs have stronger bites than smaller dogs.

Myth 3

Bully breeds are more aggressive than other dogs.

Any dog can show aggression. Research shows that aggression is not breed specific. A dog's behavior usually comes from how it is brought up, cared for, and trained.

Myth 4

Bully breeds are cute.

Bully breeds are not just cute—they are adorable! They bring joy to their families.

Glossary

breed (breed): A group of animals, within a species, that share specific physical characteristics

brindle (BRIN-dl): A pattern on an animal's coat that has colored streaks or stripes, especially in shades of brown and gray

broad (brawd): Wide from side to side

loyal (LOI-uhl): Showing or giving constant support or devotion

muscular (MUHS-kyuh-ler): Having strong, well-developed muscles. Muscles are body parts that help a person or animal move.

search-and-rescue (surch-and-res-kyoo): A specially trained group of people and animals whose job it is to find and help people who are missing or are in danger

Index

About the Author

Corinne Fickett lives in Taos, New Mexico with her husband and seven rescue dogs. She enjoys hiking in the desert and painting watercolor landscapes. Her favorite dessert is vanilla ice cream topped with chocolate syrup and rainbow sprinkles.

Written by: Corinne Fickett
Designed by: Kathy Walsh
Series Development: James Earley
Proofreader: Janine Deschenes
Educational Consultant: Marie Lemke M.Ed.

Photographs: All images from Shutterstock.

Crabtree Publishing

crabtreebooks.com 800-387-7650

In Canada: We acknowledge the financial support of the Government of Canada through the Canada Book Fund for our publishing activities.

Printed in the USA/062024/CG20240201

Published in Canada
Crabtree Publishing
616 Welland Avenue
St. Catharines, Ontario
L2M 5V6

Published in the United States
Crabtree Publishing
347 Fifth Avenue
Suite 1402-145
New York, New York, 10016

Library and Archives Canada Cataloguing in Publication
Available at Library and Archives Canada

Library of Congress Cataloging-in-Publication Data
Available at the Library of Congress

Hardcover: 978-1-0398-4466-7
Paperback: 978-1-0398-4547-3
Ebook (pdf): 978-1-0398-4620-3
Epub: 978-1-0398-4690-6
Read-Along: 978-1-0398-4760-6
Audio: 978-1-0398-4830-6